Little Children's Bible Books

ESTHER

Retold by Anne de Graaf

Illustrated by José Pérez Montero

BROADMAN
&HOLMAN
PUBLISHERS

ESTHER

Published in 2001 by Broadman & Holman Publishers,
Nashville, Tennessee

Text copyright © 2001 Anne de Graaf
Illustration copyright © 2001 José Pérez Montero
Design by Ben Alex
Conceived, designed and produced by Scandinavia Publishing House
Printed in Hong Kong
ISBN 0-8054-2193-9

Dedicated to
Pedro Pérez Rollán and Ida Marie Johanson

There once was a king of Persia who searched far and wide for a new queen. The king had the most beautiful women in the land brought to the palace. One of them would be chosen as the new queen.

7

The lucky women who were chosen waited a year to hear who had won. In the palace, they ate the best food, wore the prettiest makeup, wore the sweetest perfumes and were given the best massages.

Rub the shoulders of the person reading to you. Now it's your turn!

9

One of the girls was named Esther. She was very special, and not just because she was so beautiful. Esther was special because she was keeping a special secret. Esther's secret was that she was a Jew.

What was your most fun, all-time favorite secret? Come on, you can tell me!

When it was Esther's turn to meet
the king, there was no contest!
He chose her and she became
Queen Esther.

*Do you think the king enjoyed
choosing his new queen? Who do you
think is the best kitten on this page?*

Mordecai was Esther's cousin, but he was more like a big brother. He stood outside the palace worrying about her and asking everyone how she was. One day, Mordecai over-heard a plot to kill the king! By telling some guards about the plot, he found a way to save the king's life!

15

There was a man named Haman
who hated Mordecai because he
would not bow down to Haman.
So Haman chose a date for killing
all the Jews by throwing lots, a sort
of dice, called *Pur.*

*Haman ordered the deaths of all the
Jewish people throughout the land! So
everyone prayed to God, asking for help.
Do you pray to God when you need help?*

17

through someone else. But this could be why you are queen."

Mordecai sent a messenger to Esther with the terrible news of what Haman had ordered.

Mordecai wrote Esther, "You won't be spared because you are queen. God will save His people

Esther started praying. And she asked Mordecai and all the other Jews to also pray. For three days, everyone prayed. And then Esther went to go see the king.

Esther knew the king could have her killed for asking to see him. Would he be happy to see her?

The king smiled when he saw Esther. "Of course I will see you, Esther. What do you wish from me?" Esther said, "Would the king please come to dinner with me, and bring Haman?" The king said yes.

If you were the king or queen, what would you order for dinner every day?

At their dinner, Esther accused Haman of trying to kill all the Jews. Then she told her secret! "I am also a Jew!" When the king stepped out for a moment, Haman threw himself at her feet, begging forgiveness.

31

When the king returned, he could not believe his eyes. "Why are you bothering the queen like this? Leave her alone! Guards, arrest this evil man!"

Then the king ordered Haman hung at the same place Haman had planned to kill Mordecai.

Because Mordecai had saved the king's life, the king put Mordecai in charge of Haman's property. Then he gave Mordecai the power to issue a new order so the Jews could fight back and beat their enemies.

Who were the heroes here? Do you know a hero? Have you ever been one?

35

To celebrate, the king gave gifts to the poor. And he threw a huge party to celebrate and remember the Feast of Purim, when God used Esther the brave and beautiful to save the Jewish people.

The Feast of Purim is still celebrated to this day, all thanks to the courageous Esther, who trusted God to save her people.

A NOTE TO THE big PEOPLE:

The *Little Children's Bible Books* may be your child's first introduction to the Bible, God's Word. This book about Esther is based on passages from the Bible book by the same name. This is a DO book. Point things out and ask your child to find, seek, say, and discover.

Before you read these stories, pray that your child's little heart would be touched by the love of God. These stories are about planting seeds, having vision, learning right from wrong, and choosing to believe. Pray together after you read this. There's no better way for big people to learn from little people.

A little something fun is said in italics by the narrating animal to make the story come alive. In this DO book, wave, wink, hop, roar, or do any of the other things the stories suggest so this can become a fun time of growing closer.